THE Supreme Court and Us

CHRISTY MIHALY   ILLUSTRATED BY NEELY DAGGETT

ALBERT WHITMAN & COMPANY
CHICAGO, ILLINOIS

With special thanks to Mrs. Dunlap's 2020 fourth grade class at Yealey Elementary for their smart questions and insights; and to Wendy, Christina, and Jon for the team effort—CM

To Jamie, Kai, Iona, and Zadie, with love—ND

Library of Congress Cataloging-in-Publication data is on file with the publisher.

Text copyright © 2022 by Christy Mihaly

Illustrations copyright © 2022 by Albert Whitman & Company

Illustrations by Neely Daggett

First published in the United States of America in 2022 by Albert Whitman & Company

ISBN 978-0-8075-7664-9 (hardcover)

ISBN 978-0-8075-7665-6 (ebook)

Printed in China

10 9 8 7 6 5 4 3 2 1 WKT 26 25 24 23 22 21

Design by Aphelandra

For more information about Albert Whitman & Company, visit our website at www.albertwhitman.com.

It's true, sometimes judges send people to jail. But we judges do other things too. We can help settle arguments. Or order someone to pay money they owe.

Some judges hear appeals. If you lose your trial, you might go to a higher court— an appeals court. You can explain how the judge on the lower court was wrong.

Like if Mom says no, you can ask Gramma!

The Supreme Court is the highest court in the United States. Sometimes it decides that an appeals court made a mistake.

The Supreme Court has the last word about what United States laws mean. What the Supreme Court says goes— for the whole country.

So the Supreme Court has power. But doesn't the president have more power?

The president is in charge of only one branch of the government. The court is a separate branch. Congress is the third branch.

Branches? Like a tree?

More like a tripod.

That thing with three legs?

Right. If you took off one of those legs, the tripod would fall over.

Careful, that's my camera!

I'm the Constitution—the highest law of the land! I was written in 1787.

I set up the United States government, including the Supreme Court.

Did you say how many judges should be on the Supreme Court?

No, Congress gets to decide how many. The first US Congress passed the Judiciary Act of 1789. It said the Supreme Court would have six judges, called justices.

Congress changed the number of justices a few times after that. In 1869 a new law set the number at nine, and it hasn't changed since then.

Ha! Nine justices, so nine noses! And... ninety toes!

Wearing long robes is a tradition. For hundreds of years, judges have worn them. The robe is like a uniform.

Hmm. So judges dress alike...but do they all think alike?

No! On the Supreme Court, the justices often disagree. They discuss each case and think about it, then they vote on how to decide it.

The majority rules. One of the justices in the majority writes an opinion explaining the court's reasoning and decision.

What about the justices who lose the vote?

They can write a dissent. That's a separate opinion explaining why they think the majority is wrong about the law.

Maybe I'll try that with Mom.

I'm John Marshall. I wrote the court's decision in *Marbury v. Madison* in 1803. In that case, we looked at the Judiciary Act of 1789.

CHIEF JUSTICE JOHN MARSHALL

I remember that law. It said there were six justices.

Right! But it also did other things. Part of the law went against the Constitution. We decided that, since it was unconstitutional, we could not enforce that part.

We explained that it's the Supreme Court's job to say what the Constitution means, and to make sure the government follows it. That was a big deal.

I'm Billy Gobitis. When I was ten years old, my teacher wanted the whole class to pledge allegiance to the flag. But I refused.

Why?

In my family, we're Jehovah's Witnesses. That's our religion. We believe saying the pledge to the flag is wrong because it's like saying a prayer, or like worshipping an object.

My sister and I were kicked out of school for refusing. So we went to court.

Did you win?

No. In 1940 the Supreme Court said the school *could* require us to say the pledge.

Oh wow!

I know! Eight justices joined the opinion. They said the pledge would help students become good citizens.

That made us think hard about how our decisions affected people and how the Constitution protects the freedom of religion.

Normally, we would be guided by a case we'd recently decided. We call that following *precedent*—people need to rely on our rules when we announce them.

But this case was special. It involved the freedom of speech and freedom of religion—some of Americans' most important rights. All this helped us change our minds.

JUSTICE DOUGLAS

JUSTICE MURPHY

Also, two justices left the court after Billy's case. The two new ones who joined both believed that schools could not require students to say the pledge.

So in 1943, in our case, the court ruled that the government can't make people say something that's against their religious beliefs. We didn't have to say the pledge.

It can make a difference who the justices are!

ME COURT OF 1943

Who gets to be on the Supreme Court, anyway? Is that in the Constitution?

I don't set requirements for justices to be a certain age or have a particular education or to be born in the United States.

WE THE PEOPLE

But justices should be smart and willing to work hard. They need to work with the other justices to make difficult decisions based on the Constitution and other laws.

Famous Faces of the Supreme Court

Here are a few Supreme Court Justices you might like to know more about.

JOHN JAY was the first chief justice, or head of the Supreme Court. George Washington appointed him chief justice in 1789, and he resigned in 1795. In those six years, the court decided only four cases.

JOHN MARSHALL was the longest serving chief justice, running the court from 1801 to 1835. He worked to ensure the United States would have a strong judiciary branch.

WILLIAM HOWARD TAFT was the only person who became president of the United States (1909–1913) and then chief justice (1921–1930). Taft convinced Congress to build the Supreme Court building. Before the court moved into its own building in 1935, it used rooms in the US Capitol.

FELIX FRANKFURTER was a justice on the Supreme Court from 1939 to 1962. Born in Austria, he was the first member of the court who learned English as a second language.

THURGOOD MARSHALL, a justice from 1967 to 1991, was the first Black member of the Supreme Court. Before that, he was a lawyer who argued many Supreme Court cases on behalf of people seeking equality under the law—including *Brown v. Board of Education.*

SANDRA DAY O'CONNOR was the first woman to join the Supreme Court. She was appointed in 1981 and retired in 2006. She often cast the deciding vote when the justices voted five to four on a case.

RUTH BADER GINSBURG, the second woman and the first Jewish woman on the court, served from 1993 until her death in 2020. As a lawyer, she won many important cases securing equal rights for women, including five of the six cases she argued before the Supreme Court. She continued to work for equality as a member of the court. She became popularly known as RBG.

SONIA SOTOMAYOR was named to the court in 2009 and was the first justice of Latin American heritage. In addition to her work on the bench, she appeared (as herself) on the children's television program *Sesame Street* and wrote several books for young people.

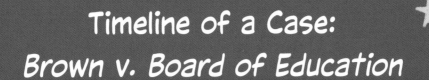

Timeline of a Case:
Brown v. Board of Education

The Supreme Court has the last word on the laws of the United States. But often the lower courts and the people of the nation spend years struggling with a difficult legal issue before the Supreme Court takes on a case. For example, here's a timeline of some of the developments leading up to the court's 1954 decision in *Brown v. Board of Education*.

1868   Fourteenth Amendment to the Constitution is ratified, stating in part: "no state shall…deny to any person the equal protection of the laws." (This clause becomes known as the Equal Protection Clause.)

1896   Supreme Court, in *Plessy v. Ferguson*, holds it is not unconsitutional for people to be separated by color—racial segregation—under a rule of "separate but equal."

1927   *Gong Lum v. Rice*: Supreme Court says a Mississippi school district can require a Chinese American girl to attend a "non-white" school instead of a "white" school under the "separate but equal" rule.

1951   *Brown v. Board of Education* case is filed in the trial court. At trial, the court decides the Topeka schools did not violate the Fourteenth Amendment, even though they maintained separate schools for white and non-white students.

1952   Arguments are held before the Supreme Court in a consolidated group of five cases from around the country, including *Brown v. Board of Education*.

1953   The members of the court are unable to reach a decision. They decide to rehear the cases. Meanwhile, the chief justice dies, and Earl Warren is named the new chief justice. The *Brown v. Board of Education* cases are reargued before the court.

1954   The court announces the unanimous ruling in *Brown v. Board of Education*, written by Chief Justice Warren. It overturns *Plessy v. Ferguson* and declares that racial segregation in public schools violates the Equal Protection Clause of the Fourteenth Amendment.

Glossary

appeal: A request to a higher court for a lower court's decision to be reversed.

brief: A written summary of the facts and law in a court case, prepared by one side of the dispute.

Constitution: The US Constitution is the written set of rules for the government; it is the highest law of the United States.

dissent: The separate opinion written by a judge who disagrees with the majority ruling, explaining the disagreement.

executive branch: The part of government that has the power to execute the laws, or put policies into effect.

freedom of religion: A person's right to practice the religion they choose without interference by the government.

freedom of speech: A person's right to state their opinions without interference by the government.

judiciary, or judicial branch: The part of government made up of the judges and courts, which has the power to interpret the laws and make sure that justice is done.

legislature, or legislative branch: The part of government that has the power to legislate, or to make laws.

precedent: A previous legal case that must be followed by the courts in later cases.

segregation: A system in which people of different races or other groups are kept separate.

unconstitutional: Going against the Constitution, or not allowed by the Constitution.

List of Cases

The cases mentioned in this book are listed below with their official citations.

Marbury v. Madison, 5 U.S. 137 (1803)
Plessy v. Ferguson, 163 U.S. 537 (1896)
Minersville School District v. Gobitis, 310 U.S. 586 (1940)
West Virginia State Board of Education v. Barnette, 319 U.S. 624 (1943)
  (The correct spelling of the family name is "Barnett," but it was misspelled by the court, so the official case name is *Barnette*.)
Brown v. Board of Education, 347 U.S. 483 (1954)
Loving v. Virginia, 388 U.S. 1 (1967)
United States v. Nixon, 418 U.S. 683 (1974)
Juliana v. United States, 947 F.3d 1159 (9th Cir. 2020)
  (In 2018, the Supreme Court issued two orders that allowed the case to proceed in the lower courts.)